One Kind of Recording,
Aphorisms

I0026935

One Kind of Recording,

Aphorisms

Laurence Musgrove

LITERARY PRESS
LAMAR UNIVERSITY

ISBN: 978-1-942956-50-1
Library of Congress Control Number:
2017960999

Illustrations: Laurence Musgrove
Manufactured in the United States of America

Lamar University Literary Press
Beaumont, Texas

For
Marie-Clare

Poetry from Lamar University Literary Press

Bobby Aldridge, *An Affair of the Stilled Heart*
Michael Baldwin, *Lone Star Heart, Poems of a Life in Texas*
Jerry Bradley, *Crownfeathers and Effigies*
Jerry Bradley and Ulf Kirchdorfer, editors, *The Great American Wise Ass Poetry Anthology*
Matthew Brennan, *One Life*
Chris Ellery, *Elder Tree*
Katherine Hoerth, *Goddess Wears Cowboy Boots*
Gretchen Johnson, *A Trip Through Downer, Minnesota*
Ulf Kirchdorfer, *Chewing Green Leaves*
Laurence Musgrove, *Local Bird*
Jan Seale, *The Parkinson Poems*
Steven Schroeder, *the moon, not the finger, pointing*
Glen Sorestad *Hazards of Eden*
Jonas Zdanys, *Red Stones*
Jonas Zdanys, *Three White Horses*

For information on these and other Lamar University Literary Press books go to www.Lamar.edu/literarypress

Writers may not be special—sensitive or talented in any usual sense. They are simply engaged in sustained use of language skills we all have. Their "creations" come about through confident reliance on stray impulses that will, with trust, find occasional patterns that are satisfying.

— William Stafford, "A Way of Writing"

There is one thought I have had, Govinda, which you will again think is jest or folly: that is, in every truth the opposite is equally true. For example, a truth can only be expressed and enveloped in words if it is one-sided.

— Herman Hesse, *Siddhartha*

Preface

Aphorists whittle sentences to a point.

When a novel is thick with character, plot and scene, the reader may be drawn quickly through the pages to keep up with the journey.

When a thin volume, like this one, includes more open space than words, there is no need to hurry.

This collection contains more than 200 aphorisms I have composed and lingered over the last 8 years or so.

I was in no hurry either.

Laurence Musgrove
San Angelo, Texas
2017

Your good friends
are good friends
to other friends, too.

He who looks
for dirt
on another
gets soiled.

Some people's problems
are solved
when someone stands near
and listens.

You can't be interested
in the truth
if you're interested only
in yourself.

You believe
we are in
the end of times
or the early days.

You see less
when you
wait and see.

The more people
you know
the more people
you know
who know the people
you know.

        Love has
        two oars:
        forgiveness
        and forgiveness.

Our backs
get tense
when our fronts
get intense.

We learn
to listen
from those
who listen
to us.

      Language
      is one kind
      of recording
      of the things
      we decide to keep.

When ready to blame,
start with yourself.

The signposts
to your life
are just up ahead
but mostly
behind you.

Freedom of choice
assumes the means
to fund the choice.
Those without
the funds to choose
assume meanness.

Depth of thinking
means nothing
if the heart
gets drowned.

Your disbelief
in the possible
doesn't make it
impossible.

Numbers don't lie.
Liars with numbers lie.

Today's review
of yesterday
will be on
tomorrow's test.

It's hard
to unbelieve a lie
you've built
so many others on.

Nepotism
is a relative
evil.

Desire deludes us
into deluding
ourselves.

Love
is pouring
your hope
into the hope
of another.

Democracy is
a fragile enemy
of wealth
and power.

Between the mind
and mindfulness
stands the body
and heart.

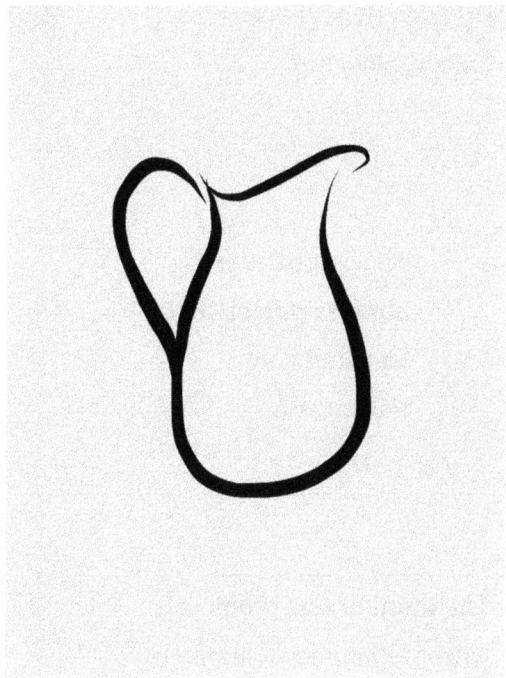

Don't confuse silence
for complacency.

The competition
always appreciates
learning how
to beat you.

The number one problem
with predictions is numbers.

Justice
is more expensive
than injustice,
but costs less.

      Always
      and never
      are twins
      of forever.

An end in itself
comes to a quick end.

It's unknown
how much of the unknown
is unknowable.

    The poem
    is a body
    filled with mind
    asking for your heart.

Are the resentful
able to resent
their resentfulness?

The more things you know
the more things remind you
of other things you know.

We study the made
to improve our making.

The fearmonger
confuses his lies
with courage.

Quality is a value
quantity can't solve for.

The best seat in the house
is sometimes outside.

The object of study
is the subject of the self.

The truth of the matter
often doesn't.

What folks lack
in responsibility,
they make up for
in blaming others.

There's no end
to the end of things
or their beginnings.

Rash decisions
make for
head scratching.

The henpecked
don't know
they're chicken.

Some writers
like getting to know
themselves
for all to read.

A memory
is an emotion
the mind can't
stop thinking.

The failure of family
is in the unforgiving.

It's hard
to look down
on those
we look up to.

After philosophy
married art,
they had a child
named literature.

Teaching is answering
the questions
anyone might have
about why anyone
should care.

Words
have no defense
against the reader,
except other words.

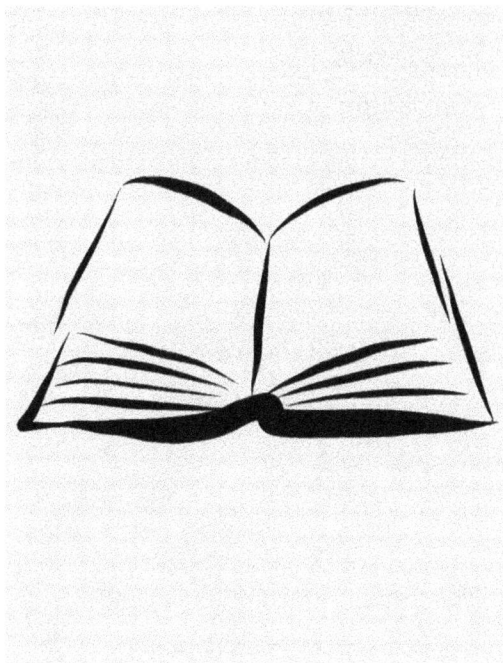

You are the artist
of the world
you occupy.

The lie is a gun
that murders the truth
on the way to power.

The more we turn others away,
the more we turn on ourselves.

Some folks
spend so much time
in their heads
their hearts go homeless.

Training in the arts
is another kind
of physical education.

Evil would be powerless
without his followers.

Rejection releases us
to be embraced by others.

The arrow
can only
fly forward
after being
pulled back.

Hiding behind hate
is a fear
that won't come out.

From the bandwagon,
it's hard to see
everyone
you're running over.

Take it or leave it
usually means take it.

The world is a school,
and a lot of people
aren't paying attention in class.

When things get out of hand,
use your hands.

Ambition and ability
are often at odds.

It must be awful
to be the one
who brings out
the worst in people.

You don't know
some folks
are itching for a fight
until you get scratched.

        Hot shots
        take pot shots.

We are bound
to be bound
to ourselves.

The problem with
looking for the best in people
is that they may think
the worst of you for it.

The hazards
of exaggeration
can't be
overemphasized enough.

The pissed-off
are frequently
shit-faced.

Even change
hasn't seen
its plans yet.

Books have spines
to give us one.

Stretching the truth
makes for thin cover.

We go into a book alone
And come out less so.

Cabbage
is a lettuce
who wanted to be
an onion.

The writer traps ideas
the reader unleashes.

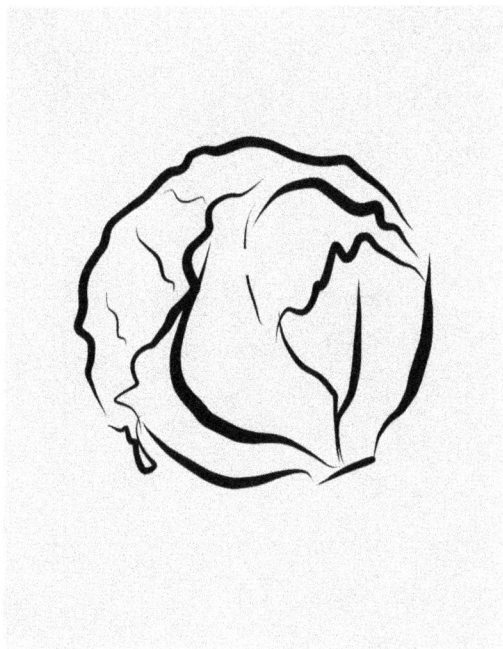

Reputation rests
on what others think
you'll do next.

The sky doesn't care
what the weather is.

Even our fears
are surprised
we're afraid.

Anger thinks
everyone is mad at him.

     The chances
     of getting it right
     the first time
     diminish significantly
     after two
     or three tries.

Politicians want
to put
someone else's money
where their mouths are.

That thing you're fighting
so hard to defend
started it first.

Desire is sustained
by the unsustainable.

The mind can't learn
until the heart is ready.

An opportunity occurs
when the present
opens a window
to let a little future in.

Uncertainty
is certain.

It's never too late
to start thinking
you should have
started earlier.

The future
has no interest
in the history
of predictions.

The body pushes.
The heart pulls.

We are
the perishable
passing on
the imperishable.

Immortality
means nothing
if there are
no mortals
to enjoy it.

Most folks
aren't very patient
unless they are
using up
other folks' time.

The impossible
is indivisible.

No door deserves
the slam it gets.

Reducing the self
to make more room
in the self for the world
enlarges the selfless world.

In a witch hunt,
the hunters are witches.

We are on loan
to one another
and the interest varies.

We were created
to create celebrations
of the creation.

Dividing people
multiplies problems.

A pear is a potato
who heard
living in the air
was sweet.

      The crooked
      will never level with you.

Let us get to know
the weeds
where we find ourselves
so often.

Dreams prove
we can see
with our eyes shut.

Nothing
is really bigger
than life.
Or death.

Here and now
come out
of nowhere.

Freedom
isn't yours
until you
dedicate
yours to
others.

Piling on is easy
until you're in the pile.

If you haven't learned it by now,
at least you learned that.

Public affairs
require private repairs.

There are no understudies.

Patience
ticks no tock.

The math of the heart
always rounds up.

If truth be told,
it could really stand
to speak up more often.

There's no reason to believe
there's no reason to believe.

The pessimist
hopes
his sneer
finds friends.

Those who rise
to the top
often forget
those holding them
up from below.

The only way
to get anywhere
is to leave.

Age is when
the temporary
becomes permanent.

Close friends
know how to
keep their distance.

After marriage,
the margin for error
is significantly reduced.

A repair shop
admits only wrecks.

A grain of truth
beats a pack of lies.

The floor will tell you
when the roof needs fixing.

The grass
is always greener
on your knees.

        The primary cause
        of miscommunication
        is words.

There'd be more to go around
if we got around more.

The imbalance
of power
never tips
toward those
who need it most.

       The failure
       of the imagination
       is not
       unimaginable.

Given
our limited abilities,
we enjoy
repeating them.

Folks
with axes
to grind
are dull.

      It's not random

      that we're creatures of
      habit.

The cutting edge
can be a bloody mess.

When push comes to shove,
try pulling on it.

All signs point to
the need for fewer signs.

Seeing eye-to-eye
beats standing toe-to-toe.

The song
you sing
sung you
first.

The body
is the oldest tool
in the shed.

Don't bite the hand
that holds yours.

When hope
succumbs to blame,
the tyranny of fear
and resentment
is victorious at last.

    Time doesn't care
    whether it takes
    control of you
    or you take
    control of it.

Anarchy promotes freedom.
Democracy promotes freedom
short of anarchy.

You can't
have a
new idea
without
having an
old one.

A writer's job
is to make readers.

Our fears
find friends
in the fears
of others.

The higher the fence,
the easier the hunt.

The more rules,
the more rulers.

Some folks
are starved
for intention.

We don't change
who we are.
We change
where we are
on the way to
who we are.

Common sense
is radical
when fear
controls the heart.

The bed has all day
for its dreams.

The third time is the charm.
The fourth is persistence.

The reader
is always
the hero
of the story.

We should love others
for their own good.

Our bodies
try to fool us
into believing
they contain us.

Creativity
is making things
out of other things.
Nobody knows
what the first thing
was made out of.

Compassion
is the compass.

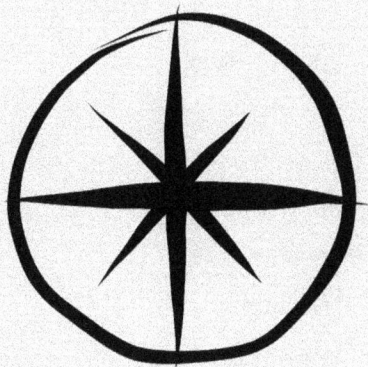

A free-for-all
is no freedom at all.

Your courage
will arrive
as soon as
the person
ahead of you
shows you
how to use it.

You are
the best question
you know.

We can empty out
the freedom in a child
or we can add to it.

Our ears
are like wings
that never gave up
on what can be found
in the air.

Compassion
is a magazine
fully subscribed
but rarely read.

The only shameful secret
is the one we can't tell.

Nature holds class
when people appear.

Sympathy is shown,
empathy is given.

Apology admits
it should have
spoken up sooner.

A shadow is seen.
Shade is felt.

Retreat
is for repair,
not defeat.

The fearful
feel fear
is a right
all should
hold dear.

Every morning,
the teacher arrives
whether we come to class
or not.

Don't fight
the storm.
Afterward,
we will have
battles enough.

Every word
is a philosophy.

The hand
that feeds us
gets to decide
what we eat.

Healing
is a wisdom
injury can't learn.

Every book
is a bible.

The page pulls
the reader in
so it can push
the reader out again.

The gap between
people and nature
is filling up with poetry.

No one
can protect you
from yourself
better than you.

An education
should blow your mind
and then help you
put it back together again.

Every picture
tells a story.
Every picture
stores a telling.

The anxiety
of the bureaucrat
is a desk disorder.

Contemplation
is a depth charge.

It's only
the string
that's stretched
that stays in tune.

Language
is a human-making
machine.

Racism
is a fascist's
favorite tool.

Opinion
has learned
to out shout fact.

Fear
has no interest
in your success.

          In Nature's
          defense,
          it got here
          first.

The singer
must listen
to sing.

Imagining
the worst possible
lets the future know
we're paying attention.

Lies
grow up
in the falsehood.

The only thing
we own
is ourselves.
Everything else
is out
to own us.

In the country
of blame,
the fault lines
run everywhere.

In turbulent times,
fear and blame
always poll high.

There's no yes in yes
until we let go of no.

The heel
is a coward.
Last one in,
first one out.

All the body is
is the only home
we'll ever have.

Self-worship
has a large
congregation.

The problem is not
that more people
own guns.
The problem is
that guns
own more people.

The wise
sound like
wiseasses
to asses.

The desire
for purity of soul
shouldn't
soil others.

Don't blame the dust
for what the wind did.

Our lives depend
on those who
depend on us.

Our differences
are planted in
what we share.

Ignorance
is the persistent ignoring
of what's often taught freely.

The side
to take is
common
ground.

To know yourself
is to know
when to say no
to yourself.

We believe
despair is
more inevitable
than hope.
Or not.

Anger lets
violence think
it's courage.

If you are loyal
to the right ideas,
the right people
will be loyal to you.

What's
in us
was made
by what's
in others.

Greed is a beast
with claws and teeth
reckless for
what isn't his.

Truth can live
without us.

The tyrant
arrives
when democracy
fails.

You're no good
for others
if you're no good
to yourself.

Education should
encourage in us
a brave heart,
a ready mind,
a wide embrace.

Your primary
assignment
in freedom
is to make
it for others.

If we can't
stand to look
at ourselves,
we'll never
stand up
for ourselves.

We seek
to confront
our ignorance
or not.

Lack of judgment
means
you can't see it
in others
either.

The aphorism
is a song
we've never heard
but recognize.

Despair's
only enemy
is that hope
you're standing
there holding.

Herding
is a form
of communication
dogs also use
on people.

Aphorists
whittle
sentences
to a point.

Inexperience
is discovered
in experience.

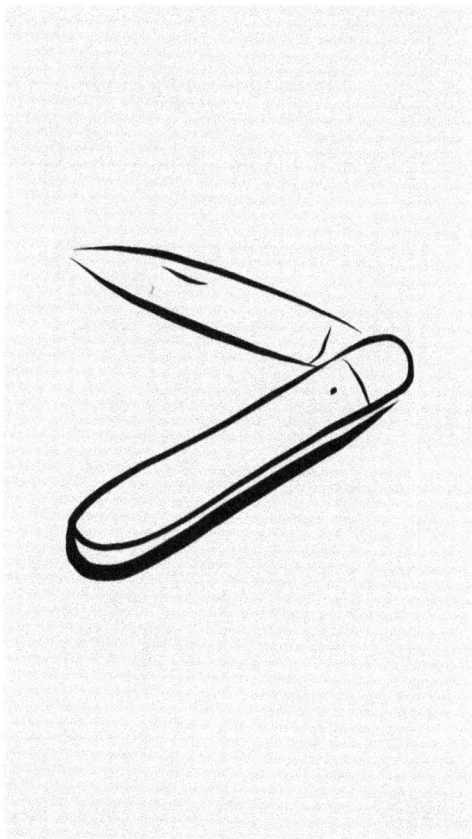

Author of the poetry collection *Local Bird*, Laurence Musgrove is professor of English at Angelo State University where he teaches creative writing, literature, drawing to learn, comics, and mindful-ness. His poems have appeared in *Southern Indiana Review, Concho River Review, descant, Elephant Journal, Inside Higher Ed, Buddhist Poetry Review, Journal of the Assembly for Expanded Perspectives on Learning, Southwestern American Literature, Ink Brick,* and *New Texas.* He is also co-editor with Terry Dalrymple of the anthology *Texas Weather*, a collection of poetry, fiction, and nonfiction on the power and beauty of weather in the Lone Star State.

www.ingramcontent.com/pod-product-compliance
Lightning Source LLC
Chambersburg PA
CBHW022341280326
41934CB00006B/729